Winter

Signs of the Season
Around North America

Written by Mary Pat Finnegan   Illustrated by Jeremy Schultz

Content Advisor: Julie Dunlap, Ph.D. • Reading Advisor: Lauren A. Liang, M.A.
Literacy Education, University of Minnesota, Minneapolis, Minnesota

PICTURE WINDOW BOOKS
MINNEAPOLIS, MINNESOTA

To Grady and Casey—Winter adventurers and hibernators extraordinaire!—M.P.F.

The author would like to thank Professor Walkie Charles and Professor Steven Jacobson of the Alaska Native Languages Center at the University of Alaska, Fairbanks; Nora Murdock, Ecologist with the Appalachian Highlands Network of the National Park Service; John Finnegan with the North Carolina Natural Heritage Program; and Wilma Payne, teacher in the Iditarod Area School District, McGrath, Alaska.

Editor: Nadia Higgins
Designer: Melissa Voda
Page production: The Design Lab
The illustrations in this book were prepared digitally.

Picture Window Books
5115 Excelsior Boulevard
Suite 232
Minneapolis, MN 55416
1-877-845-8392
www.picturewindowbooks.com

Printed in the United States of America.
1 2 3 4 5 6 08 07 06 05 04 03

Library of Congress Cataloging-in-Publication Data
Finnegan, Mary Pat, 1961–
  Winter : signs of the season around North America / written by Mary Pat Finnegan ; illustrated by Jeremy Schultz.
    p. cm. — (Through the seasons) Includes index.
  Summary: Examines how winter brings observable changes in weather, nature, and people.
  ISBN 1-4048-0001-8 (lib. bdg. : alk. paper)
  1. Winter—North America—Juvenile literature. [1. Winter.] I. Schultz, Jeremy, ill. II. Title. III. Through the seasons (Minneapolis, Minn.)
  QB637.8 .F55 2003
  508.2—dc21   2002005838

One way to mark the seasons is by looking at the calendar. The calendar dates are based on Earth's yearly trip around the sun. In North America, winter begins on the shortest day of the year, either December 21 or 22. Throughout the winter, the days keep getting longer.

Another way to mark the seasons is to look around you at the changes in weather and nature. In North America, the first signs of winter appear in the north, then move south. This book helps you to see the signs of winter in different places around North America.

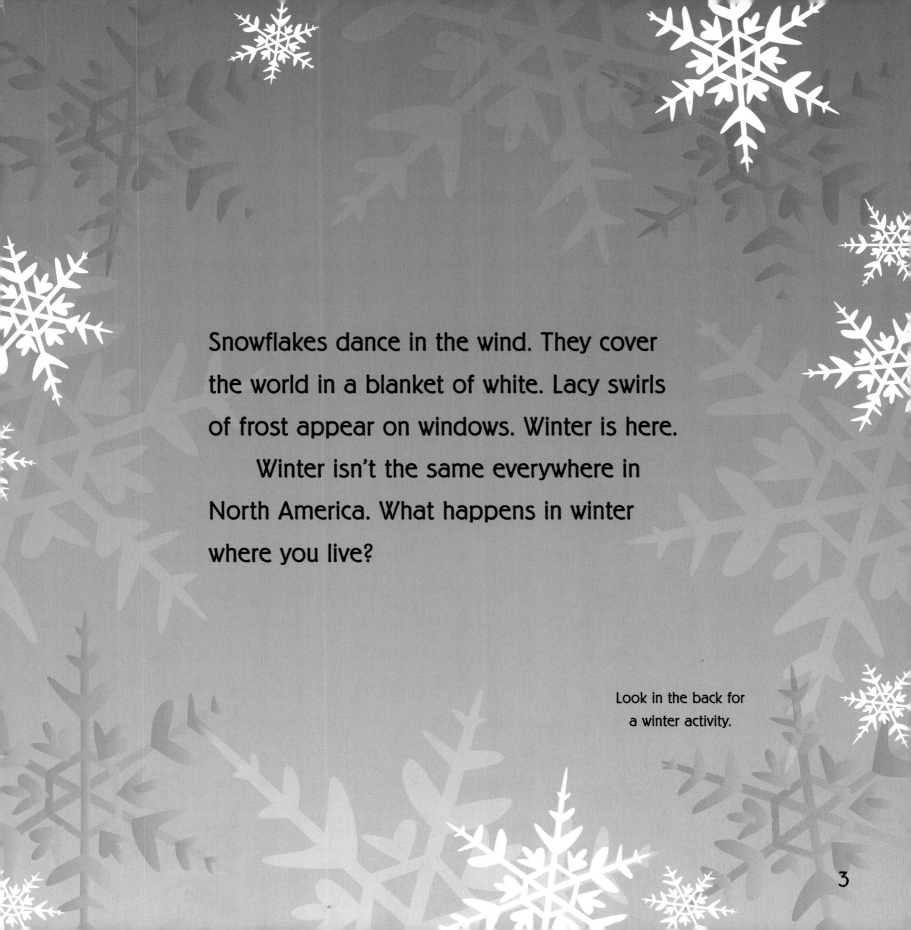

Snowflakes dance in the wind. They cover the world in a blanket of white. Lacy swirls of frost appear on windows. Winter is here.

Winter isn't the same everywhere in North America. What happens in winter where you live?

Look in the back for
a winter activity.

4

Snow sparkles in the moonlight—
but it's early afternoon! In Alaska
and northern Canada, many places
do not see the sun for weeks.

During these cold, dark days
you can sometimes see an amazing
light show in the sky. The northern
lights look like waving ribbons of
green, red, and purple.

5

In New England, it sometimes snows so much that children don't have to go to school. Snow days mean lots of fun outside. Fall back into a snowbank and wave your arms and legs. You've made a beautiful snow angel!

Here comes a snowplow to clear the roads.

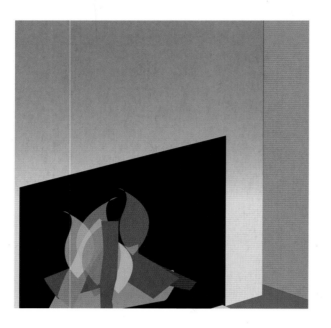

Brrrr! It's too cold to play outside at night. Winter evenings are the perfect time to read a story, play board games, or sit by a fire and drink hot chocolate.

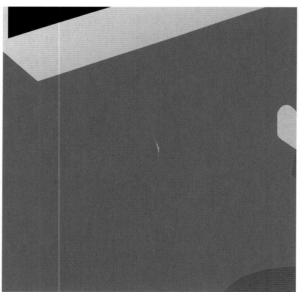

Many animals spend the winter in a deep sleep.
They hibernate in their dens, nests, and burrows.

FUN FACT:
Hibernating animals can go for a long
time without eating. Animals that do not
hibernate have to work hard to find food
in winter. Some of them eat food that
they stored away in autumn.

In the Midwest, thick ice covers lakes and ponds. People fish through holes they have drilled in the ice. Some people bring little houses onto the ice so they can keep warm while they fish.

FUN FACT:
Lake ice should be at least four inches (10 centimeters) thick before you walk on it.

Farmers are happy to see a thick blanket of snow cover the fields. In spring, it will melt into the ground and give plants the water they need.

It's time to go sledding. The wind stings your face as you speed down the hill.

Chickadee-dee, chickadee-dee-dee. Can you hear the call of the chickadee? Look at the red cardinal sitting on a branch. Chickadees and cardinals stay in the Midwest all winter, while most other birds fly to warmer places.

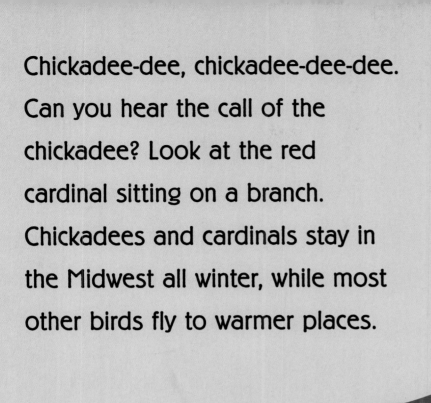

FUN FACT:
Chickadees have to eat a lot in winter to stay alive. On very cold days, they eat 20 times more food than they do in the summer.

Winter in the Appalachian Mountains is damp and chilly. Watch your step. On the ground, frosty fallen leaves cover rocks and acorns. It feels as if you're walking on marbles.

Bare tree branches make dark shapes against the sky. Pine trees stand tall against winter winds. A flying squirrel sails from tree to tree, its long tail trailing behind it. It looks like a kite.

Winter is warm and sunny in parts of California. The orange groves are buzzing with activity. It's harvest time.

16

Lettuce, broccoli, and carrots are ready for picking, too.
The fresh fruits and vegetables are packed and shipped
to grocery stores in colder places.

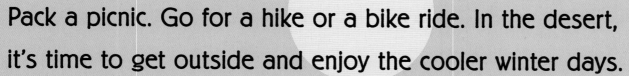

Pack a picnic. Go for a hike or a bike ride. In the desert, it's time to get outside and enjoy the cooler winter days.

18

At night, paper lanterns light sidewalks and welcome visitors.

19

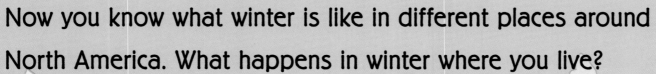

Now you know what winter is like in different places around North America. What happens in winter where you live?

FUN FACT:
Winter is the time for many celebrations, including Christmas, Hanukkah, and Kwanzaa. The first day of January marks the beginning of a new year. In February, Valentine's Day is a special day for showing others how much they mean to us.

ALASKA/NORTHERN CANADA

Fairbanks, Alaska
Average high January temperature: 0°F/-18°C
Hours of daylight on January 1st: 4 hours, 3 minutes
What to wear: parka, snow pants, hat, earmuffs, heavy boots, and mittens
Signs of winter: dark days and lots of snow and ice

NEW ENGLAND

Portsmouth, New Hampshire
Average high January temperature: 32°F/0°C
Hours of daylight on January 1st: 9 hours, 4 minutes
What to wear: winter coat, hat, boots, and mittens
Signs of winter: skiing, sledding, icicles

MIDWEST

Minneapolis/St. Paul, Minnesota
Average high January temperature: 21°F/-6°C
Hours of daylight on January 1st: 8 hours, 51 minutes
What to wear: long underwear, woolly sweater, winter coat, scarf, hat, boots, and mittens
Signs of winter: ice-fishing houses, snowmen

APPALACHIAN MOUNTAINS

Asheville, North Carolina
Average high January temperature: 48°F/9°C
Hours of daylight on January 1st: 9 hours, 49 minutes
What to wear: winter coat, hat, boots, and mittens
Sign of winter: ice forming along the edges of streams, rivers, lakes, and ponds

CALIFORNIA

Sacramento, California
Average high January temperature: 53°F/12°C
Hours of daylight on January 1st: 9 hours, 32 minutes
What to wear: jacket and a warm sweater on chilly evenings
Sign of winter: workers picking oranges and other fruits and vegetables on farms

DESERTS

Nogales, Mexico
Average high January temperature: 63°F/17°C
Hours of daylight on January 1st: 10 hours, 9 minutes
What to wear: light jacket
Sign of winter: a large cactus decorated with Christmas tree lights

Make a Winter Treat for Birds

You Will Need:

An adult

A pinecone

A piece of string about 18 inches ($1/2$ meter) long

Peanut butter

A spatula or knife

Birdseed on a plate

Tie the string around the top of the pinecone. Use the spatula or knife to spread peanut butter all over the pinecone. Roll the pinecone in the birdseed. Have an adult help you tie the pinecone to a tree branch. Watch the birds eat the delicious treat!

Words to Know

Hanukkah—a Jewish holiday. Lighting the menorah, a special candleholder, celebrates a miracle when God kept one day's worth of oil burning for eight days.

harvest time—the time of year when fruits and vegetables are ready for picking

hibernate—to spend the winter in a deep sleep

Kwanzaa—a celebration of African-American history, culture, and values. Kwanzaa lasts from December 26 to January 1.

winter—the season between autumn and spring. In North America, winter starts in late December and finishes at the end of March.

To Learn More

AT THE LIBRARY

Branley, Franklyn Mansfield. *Snow Is Falling.* New York: HarperCollins, 2000.

Rylant, Cynthia. *Poppleton in Winter.* New York: Blue Sky Press, 2001.

Schaefer, Lola M. *A Snowy Day.* Mankato, Minn.: Pebble Books, 2000.

Stille, Darlene R. *Winter.* Minneapolis: Compass Point Books, 2001.

Wilson, Karma. *Bear Snores On.* New York: Margaret K. McElderry Books, 2001.

ON THE WEB

U.S. Naval Observatory
http://www.usno.navy.mil
For sunrise and sunset times in cities around the world

National Oceanic and Atmospheric Administration Education Resources
http://www.education.noaa.gov
Activities, safety tips, and articles on weather for teachers and students

Want to learn more about winter? Visit FACT HOUND at *http://www.facthound.com.*

Index